瑜伽修行語錄

Sayings

雖然默默無言，卻又道盡一切

Saying nothing says it all

斯瓦米韋達・帕若堤 Swami Veda Bharati —— 著　　石宏 —— 譯

譯後感言

　　斯瓦米韋達生前將他處於靜默中所湧現的精句，收集為一本小冊，提名為「Sayings」。按，Saying 有諺語、格言、箴言的意思。他講過的一些名言，例如「靜默時才言語」、「斷食中方進食」都收錄在其中（請讀者不要讀漏其中的「才」和「方」，少了這一個字，整個句子的意義就有所不同）。

　　書中，每隔幾段斯瓦米韋達就會提醒讀者，留心閱讀書頁中空白的部分，這就是他在提點我們要做的工夫。我們尋常的習慣都是把注意力放在「突出」的現象上，而不注意背景。例如夜深人靜之際浴室傳來滴水聲，注意力就容易被聲響所帶走而讓人輾轉難眠。斯瓦米韋達會說：「你為什麼要去聽滴水聲，而不去傾聽每一滴水聲之間的寧靜？」他又說：「西方的油

畫是要把畫布上每一方寸都塗上油墨，而中國的水墨畫則是墨水畫到之處和留白之處同樣重要。」

滴水之間的寧靜，就是畫中的留白，就是紙上字與字之間的空距，就是呼與吸交替間剎那的停頓。抓住那，就能帶我們入靜，覺察到自己內在本已有之的那份靜默。當然，短暫覺知到淺層的靜默不難。難的是維持住覺知，難的是入到深層的靜默。所以還是需要習練瑜伽或者任何禪定功夫才能得力，才能更上層樓，才能潛入心識汪洋至寧靜的深處。

閱讀本書時，斯瓦米韋達建議讀者要慢慢咀嚼，默默沉思，如此才能得益。您下次出門遠行時，與其帶本厚重的長篇小說，何妨帶上這本書為伴？

——石宏

目次

匍伏於

至尊上師跟前

他

默默無言

卻又道盡一切

前言

　　長久以來，有種神祕現象一直讓我深思不已：為什麼在靜默沉思時，反而有那麼多的字句會像泉湧似的浮現，讓人非要說出來不可？我把其中一部分收集在這本集子裡，希望你會喜歡。

　　這些字句是不請自來，自然浮上心頭的。如果有人自作主張把珍貴的珠寶、玉石，連同石塊、石子送到別人家的門口，該怎麼處理呢？我現在也自作主張，把這些送到你家門口。對不起，我沒有先把石頭從珠寶中撿出去。

　　這些字句是需要慢慢咀嚼，默默沉思的。一句一句地讀。讓它們的情懷留在心頭猶若「俳句」，把問題留下來當作「公案」。迷惑就由它迷惑。直到內心輕聲說，明白了。這裡的文字要表達的，不是它們表面的意義。若山峰不是

山峰，谷底不是谷底，究竟是什麼？「女人」不是指在女性的身子，因為我們這些出家人是沒有性別觀念的。那麼，所謂「女人」究竟是什麼意思？杉樹在問「如何」是什麼意思，茉莉花樹輕聲質疑什麼是「為什麼」的定義，他們目的何在？這裡有一場又一場的禪思法會，我邀請你來參加。在不知不覺中（注意，是不知不覺地），你的行為舉止就會不同。

請你也務必要「讀」書中刻意留白的地方。留白也是字句，是老師在斷食和靜語的期間送給學生的語句。

這裡有任何珍貴的，都來自我們的傳承。那些一文不值的石子，則是來自於我。

——斯瓦米韋達・帕若堤

寫出來的字與字之間的空白，是呼吸之間的停頓。
你要學會去讀那些「印」出來的留白。

時間跟你一樣也是人，
可以跟他打商量的。

要盡快達到目的，
就往相反的方向走。

要求勝？
先俯首稱臣。

僵硬的其實脆弱而易碎。
柔軟的才耐久，有韌性而堅強。

白天和黑夜都是神造的。
為什麼你必定只能挑一個？

遇上矛盾局面，要在對立的兩難之間做出選擇，
不妨二者都選；
同時有著南北極，你就會成為一塊磁鐵。

懂得「多」是無知；
只知道「一」才是智慧。

帶著欲望之人撫摸的是肢體。
有愛之人撫摸的是心靈。
去愛。

能做個女性，就不必再學別的。
花朵何必去追尋石頭的身分。

如果你是男人，學習變得女性。
如果你是女人，保持女性。

重大災難
是為了替再生開路
而做出的再調整。

懂了這個道理，你就能像
風雨夜後冒出來的一朵鮮花。

若妲嬉笑間可以變為奎師那。
奎師那不能扮盡若妲的角色。

細微的傲慢最能作惡；
我們不知道它埋伏在哪裡。
找到它，磨光它。

自己的歡樂應該來自能夠帶歡樂給他人。
要求別人回報歡樂，就會抵銷你已付出的。

不要老是數你收到多少禮。
應該只記著你欠了多少。

去學細微身的舞步。

譯注：奎師那（Krishna）是印度的神，若妲（Radha）是他的妻子。

想克服恐懼？
就停止導致任何生靈的死亡。
即使是一隻螞蟻，也要視之如親人。

走到哪裡，都要把你心靈的芳香散發出去。

所有空間中，無非是神的歡笑聲
也讓你的笑聲，加入其中。

有人行將變得不友善之際，
對他友善。

不要與別人競爭，
你只要盡力就好。

在瑞斯凱詩，我們為你的衣服染色。
可是我們只用藏紅花色。

經常做點無用之事
例如微笑，例如靜坐。

學會去讀印在留白之處的東西。

太使勁只會失敗。
你有太使勁嗎？

動起來要猶若毫不出力。
滑動。流動。

先把別人可能對你不滿之處說出來，
那麼他們就無話可說。

每當你有股不由自主的衝動，要一吐為快的時候，
那正是你一定要保持靜默的時候。

沒有調節不了的衝突。

我應該抓住這機會，還是放過它？
是的。

這是白的，還是黑的？
是的。

這是邪，還是正？
是的。

真相究竟是這樣的，還是那樣的？
是的。

若你被兩難的煎熬局面所苦，
這正表示你錯過了
可以兼容並蓄的第三條路
能讓 $3 = 1$。

欲望其實是過去經驗
所遺留下來的記憶。
老是重複做同樣的事,
難道不無聊嗎?

我信的宗教是對的還是錯的？
是的。

不要去壓抑憤怒。
只要，不生它。

再重複一次，要懂得去讀紙上
空白處所印的是什麼。

不要只為了感覺自己的高大，
而與侏儒結伴。

放縱，就是被打敗了。

能克制，就是勝利。

除非你能視工作為樂趣，否則不要工作。
祝你做得開心。

保持快樂，不用理由，
沒有原因，時時如此。

比快樂更快樂的是
寧靜。

你懂了去讀紙上留白之處
所印的東西嗎？

狂喜微不足道，不若寧靜。

前一頁留白之處，你可以看見寧靜。

就在那裡沉思吧。

啜飲一小口橙汁
就能送你進入神祕的狂喜；
只要專注地啜飲。

「出」和「入」之間有個停頓，
那是敞開的大門，能通往永恆。

什麼是塵世？
有限

如何是超越塵世？
無限。

哪怕再小的一顆火苗，也無懼於
最大廳中最厚重的黑暗。

你不用試著去求知一切。
要傾盡全力，止於能知那「一切」。

能帶領你找到自己的人，
是你該依附在他足下的大師。

無論你在上一個留白得到什麼印象，
凝視它，沉思之。

岸流，則河不流。

富人雖吃得多，嚐到的少。
窮人卻吃得少，而嚐到的多。
後者更富有。

今天我有過一次
可怕的瀕死經驗：
有三口氣之久，
我忘了把祈禱織入呼吸中。
其後，我又重獲新生。

意欲登上山頂，
先下到谷底
你就會處於巔峰。

智慧不用多字。

上一個空白處的靜默，你做了嗎？

微風不需要護照；
呼吸中的人類不需要國籍。

黃金時代何時重臨？
就你而言，決定權在你。

即使在黃金時代，可能有人還是活在自己的黑暗期。
儘管在黑暗期，也有人可以活在自己的黃金時代。

你想在神之前隱身？
你是想讓波浪不濕嗎？

你想躲過神？
你是想讓火花不帶火嗎？

你想否定神的存在？
你是想讓光否認太陽嗎？

不要去求當那折損花草的暴風。
求做那能吸取芬芳的微波。

想要孩子聽你的？
先跪下來，讓你的眼睛
和他的臉高度一樣，
然後一字一句清楚地說，
輕柔地說。

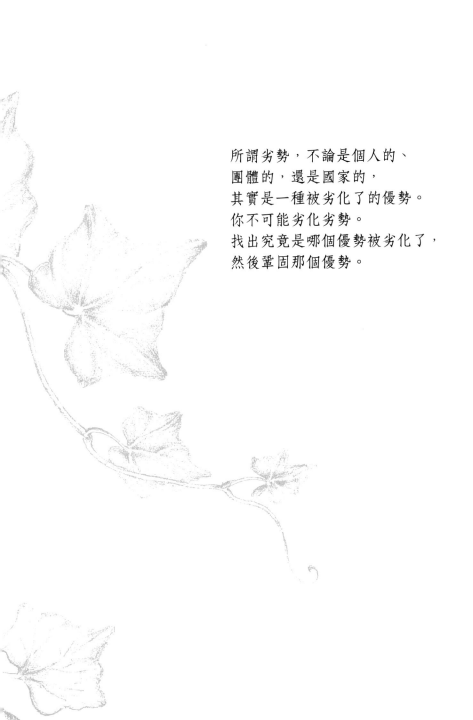

所謂劣勢，不論是個人的、
團體的，還是國家的，
其實是一種被劣化了的優勢。
你不可能劣化劣勢。
找出究竟是哪個優勢被劣化了，
然後鞏固那個優勢。

上一個留白之處，是呼吸間的停頓。
你已經用自我觀察、用覺知，
把它填滿了。

有人說「我不信神」嗎？
太妙了。
多虧神的恩賜，至少這人說了「神」這個字。
句子其他的部分無關緊要。

在憤怒之際，不可以去責罵孩子。
待平靜了，才假裝去責罵。

我見過有人試著用掃帚把黑暗從房間裡掃出去。
結果連一根最小的蠟燭都沒點。

我見過有人被憤怒的人激怒。
我說：應該對憤怒感到憤怒，然後消滅它。

格利佛來到一個城市，當地的宗教不允許
吃任何甜味的食物。他們說，我們不能吃你帶來的糖，
可是請為我們形容一下「甜」的滋味。

格利佛來到一座島嶼，當地人遵循聖經的教導：
「讓你們的眼睛如一。」
所以嬰兒一出生就被蒙上一隻眼睛，終生不掀開。
他們請格利佛形容一下，用一雙眼看到的世界是怎麼樣的。

「神」這個字在嘴中是什麼滋味？
至甜美不過。

譯注：格利佛（Gulliver）是西方童話故事《格利佛遊記》中的主角。

瑜伽大師來到凡世。
凡人的第三眼都被蒙住了。
他們拒絕掀開自己被蒙住的眼睛，
卻問他，三隻眼能看到的實相是怎樣的？

當神造了靈魂，
祂需要有個地方讓它住。
因此祂打造了心靈。

除非你能把工作當成是在度假，否則就什麼都不做。
盡情享受度假！

用三隻眼睛看到的世界是什麼樣的？
沒有三度空間，也沒有被四個角圍起來的正方形。

抱歉，我在下一個空間什麼也寫不進去，
那裡已經太滿了。
所以，請欣賞它的充實，在那裡多待一會兒。

恨對愛說：我恨你。
愛對恨說：我愛你。

即使是最嚴肅的事，也要嬉戲於其中。

心是天地間最純潔、最清晰、
最明亮、最平和的地方。
所以神讓靈魂住在心靈中。

心靈有如海洋。
表面有風雨，深處最平靜。

灰塵在水晶上可以被看得清清楚楚。
我們的污點會在心靈上現形。

讓你心靈中的水晶燈長明。

3

為什麼要被那永遠填不滿的欲望所折磨？
該享受節欲所帶來的至樂。

上一頁的畫是我見過最美的。
盡情欣賞吧。

不要被寂寞所苦；享受孤寂。

如何從一己的牢籠逃出去？
走進寺院的牢籠，活在孤寂的靜默中。

寺院的牢籠就在你心中。
進去吧。

不要再用馬不停蹄的旅行來消耗自己。
做個朝聖者。

大地再大，容不下兩位大帝。
一床被子雖小，也夠兩名苦行僧人同眠。
求知足。

假如星座能知我的命運，
能知星座命運的是誰呢？
我寧願直接向祂求教我的命運。

當我向神問我的命運，
祂說：以你的所作所為，來創造你自己的命運。

你要神做你的牧者？
那麼，先把自己當作一隻羔羊吧。

一小口節欲帶來的充實感
遠勝於縱欲之洋。

報名參加靜止比賽。
不用爭，你就會贏。

為何要為飢餓所苦？
享受斷食的樂趣吧。

足以填滿海洋的傲慢，
比不上些許的謙遜。

放空你所學，智慧自然來。

愚人常比飽學之士更有智慧。

靜坐時不要和別人攀比。
要獨處。

不要加入閒談哲理的團體。
保持靜默。

與無知的人相伴，要顯得愚昧。

與無信仰的人相伴，要祕密去愛。

助人而不讓人知是你在相助。
你助人的能力將會提升。

為人治病而不為人知是你在治。
你治病的能力將會更強。

英文字母「S」的發音，
即使在「鹹海」（salt see）這個名詞中，
聽起來仍然是又柔又甜。
即使處在最嚴峻、最狂暴的時刻，
仍然要又柔又甜。

若你見到兩人在爭吵，
就對著他們微笑，
什麼也不用說。
氣氛就會變得不同。

有人對你皺眉，就報以微笑。

在往山上倒流的河中行舟。

智慧的曙光在夜半來到。

一個個字母都是從天使的號角傳出來的音符。
讓有耳朵的人去聽吧。

即使是帶刺的灌木，蜜蜂採到的就只是蜜。

有些雲隆隆作聲，有些降雨。
做那能降雨的雲。

如果你能製造奇蹟，要默默地做。
事後否認那是你所做。

給人忠告，要不落忠告的痕跡，人家才會聽從。
領導他人，要不著領導的痕跡，人家才會服從。

螞蟻所馱的象，是生了翅膀的。
蚊蟲所吞的天，是成了無邊的。
祈禱，願自己成為那象、那天。

如果社會風氣視酒為神聖之物，
聖人就把水變成酒。
如果不是酒，是奶，聖人就把水變成奶。
我們從這兒學到什麼？

昨夜睡眠中，
你是否聽到花園中花苞綻放為玫瑰的聲音，
而且，月亮為此高聲叫好，眾星也在歡笑慶祝？
那表示你靜坐的功夫已經純熟了。

卡比爾說：螞蟻能駝象，蚊蟲能吞天。
如果你見到這景象，保持靜默，
你就會成為那螞蟻、那蚊蟲。

譯注：卡比爾（Kabir）是十六世紀印度詩人哲學家。

開悟這檔事被拖得夠久了。
現在，不要再推拖。

在黑夜中有人朝你走來，你感到害怕，
但他也同樣怕你。能讓他不怕你，
你就能征服自己一切的恐懼。

當你能連續十二口氣不停頓，
做到向內呼氣，向外吸氣，
那就表示你已經進入了那個「大蓄水池」。

有些門，關才是開，而開才是關。
要學會由這樣的門進入。

神為了自娛，就弄了場魔術、演了齣鬧劇，名叫宇宙。
你卻如此把它當真。

烏龜能放鬆，所以贏了賽事。
兔子急躁，所以輸了。

聖者靜默，所以千年之後的世界仍然在聽他。
多舌之人，瞬間就被遺忘。

刻意不留名，反而永遠被記住。

我已經告訴你這麼多東西。
哪天你找到了神為祂自己取的祕密名字，
請務必要告訴我。

在上一個留白處，
你有聽到自己靈魂的寧靜嗎？

要採智慧的珍珠，就得深潛。

最聰明的人也有愚蠢的時候。
可不要誤把他們的愚蠢當作智慧。

愚人也有流露出大智慧的時候。
不要輕率地斥他們的智慧為愚蠢。

看起來愚蠢的，有時反而是智慧的。
要有判斷力。

在一齣戲中，丑角是重要角色。
在神的宇宙裡，我們的重要性也是如此。

神是做什麼的？祂作詩。
祂寫了什麼？宇宙詩篇。

把呼吸放慢。你急什麼？

對子宮不敬的人，是僵硬之人。

向你人性的基本欲望讓步吧。
例如，施捨！

向你人性的基本欲望讓步吧。
例如，犧牲！

在夏日，開心享受，
把太陽的能量儲存起來。
在冬日，開心享受，
冷靜下來，
讓新陳代謝慢下來，
就可以活久一些。

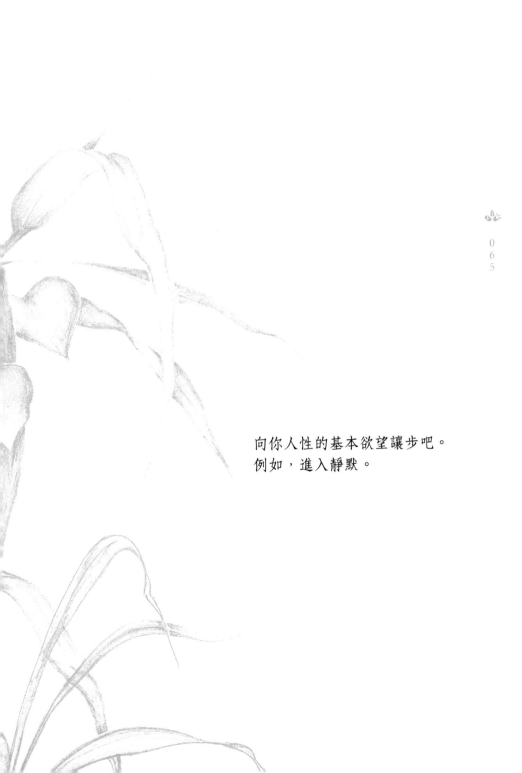

向你人性的基本欲望讓步吧。
例如，進入靜默。

好極了，你剛才靜默了一會兒。

不要硬得像塊岩石。要強韌如水，水可以磨石成沙。
學習為水之道，亦即女性之道。

如果你非要結束一段關係，
不要給對方痛苦，也不要一直扛著痛苦。

如果你非要結束一段關係，
不要留下沒有還清的業債。

礦藏是為了裝飾自己而產玉石嗎？
葡萄乾是為了品嚐自己才變甜嗎？
高貴之人都是為人，低劣之人則是為己。

你跌在泥濘中，就別期望能
撐著泰姬陵的大理石地板站起來。
你要將手放進泥濘中，才能起身。

要晉身為神的信徒，
你就先要成為世人眼中至愚之人。

如果世人以為你有智慧，
你就還不算是個信徒。

要實踐無為，你就要百分百積極任事。
——引自《薄伽梵歌》

做個縱情享受的老饕。
細細品嚐神的滋味。

如果有人問你，神是……
……就把祂的沉默倒進他們的耳中。

你要精於懶惰之藝。
坐下。就坐著，四肢都不要動。
就連心都不讓它奔馳。
誓言懶惰，就忠於所誓。

愚人才是聰明人。神將一切關懷都給了他們。

追隨神太難了──你以為。
活在世上就容易嗎？

去追尋從容的人生，從容如神。

你有在上個留白處拾階而上嗎？
步步高升的感覺如何？

凡是你所追尋的，會背著你而逃。
凡是你所逃避的，會追著你而來。

你害怕什麼，就正面迎向它。
你所怕的、你的恐懼心，反而會怕你。

有為自己找樂子之樂，也有為別人帶來歡樂之樂。
兩者之間，從後者得來的樂更為強烈。

即使是牢騷，只要是對著神而發的，
也可以變成祈禱。
對神去發一頓牢騷，試試看。

神要救的人，就是祂所毀的人。
求毀於神之手吧。

神是慈母的奶水，叫作智慧之白光。

不要怕去愛，
就怕不去愛。

若你眼中有光，
就能點亮你的整個世界。

每週做一日靜默，
許你能一窺永恆。

不能謙下請人恕己，
也定不能寬以恕人。

把心中的皺紋抹平，
臉面自然光滑到老。

若你聽得到自己心中的靜默，
就聽不到外界的噪音。

在前面空白之處，你聽到你心中的靜默嗎？

愛，融在平衡的狀態中，有如聖餐。
愛，沒有平衡的情緒，就成了毒藥。
願你的杯中沒有毒藥。

不能視神為友，就與祂為敵，向祂挑戰。
祂會接受你的挑戰，那你至少
有機會面對面見祂一次。

5

日常都有許多空白的時刻，
碰到時，不要忘了有些是該用來靜默的。

在上一頁的留白處，你曾否在那往上逆流的瀑布中沐浴？
所有靜默都是往上逆流的瀑布。
多多沐浴其中。

封鎖的心，會把開闊的空間視為囚牢。
解脫了的聖人，即使被囚禁，
也能將典獄長們從他們的囚牢中解放出來。
不要躋身於囚徒中，要躋身為解放者。

害怕影子嗎？
就到有遮陰之處休息。

每個飛轉的輪子都有一個絕對靜止的中心。
倦了團團轉？
那就到中心處休息。

弟子的哥哥是個酒鬼，不肯去見大師。
大師在他的隱居處掛上招牌，寫著：
「酒館」
哥哥去了，就被感化。

你的酒館什麼時候開張？

心要去什麼地方，就讓它去，因為神在那裡。

心之所在就是神之所在，就讓心在神之中休息。

去內在的世界旅遊。
去「內觀」。

呱噪的心，去到寧靜的森林，
能把擾攘留在腦後。
而靜逸的人，可以讓鬧市靜下來。

樂是苦的解藥。
在苦中，就造樂吧。

不要煩惱有什麼不樂的。
享受有什麼可樂的。

站在湖邊，你覺得錯過了海，
那你也錯過了湖的樂趣。

雕刻家從不雕刻；他們只是
用雕刻刀剷去那些蓋住了所要展露的部分。
剷去吧，讓你要過的人生、你要的美，得以展露。

在暴風下就不要站得像一棵高大的樹，
你會被連根拔起。

天真是最高的智慧。

在洪流前要像蘆葦一樣彎下腰，
你才能留下來。

不防衛，才是最佳的防衛之道。

只有謙虛，才能保住自尊。

你身陷在風暴之中？
保持靜止。
風暴終將遠離。

即使是高大如山之人，
在神的跟前只是侏儒。

你最初是住在母親之內。
如是觀想
可以悟出處理情緣的智慧。
你曾經住在你母親「之內」。

靈魂是死亡之手所搆不到的。
唯有明白這個道理的人，
才能掙脫對死亡的恐懼。

能運用一萬種語言來辯論的學者
在那「全知者」面前，也只是一個文盲。

就算你有三萬六千「神年」壽命，
你仍舊活在死亡的恐懼中。

針才會舞動，磁鐵是靜止的。
「被動」的磁石，才能動外物。

受風暴翻騰的大海，其下二十呎就是靜止的。
心也是如此。

潛入你的心中。

與人相處，想贏，你就先輸了。
先輸，你反而贏。

鏡中人以為你是他的倒影。

如果你的眼神能表達愛，
你會需要其他飾物嗎？

只要心念是美麗的，即使最其貌不揚的人
也會是最有吸引力的人。

玫瑰叢把芳香的花瓣散落在你行走的路徑上，
你曾否彎下腰來對它道謝？

如果是為了金錢才工作，
就都是在賣淫。
工作是為了服務奉獻。
接受金錢是因為有需要。
二者之間沒有關聯。

心無關緊要，
靈才是。

身無關緊要，
呼吸才是。

物質無關緊要，
精神才是。

雲不吃它所滋養的穀子；
樹不吃它所生長的果子；
河流不為了自己的利益而帶來甘泉。
偉人不需要任何理由，只是為了眾生而活。
——梵文諺語

糟了！我忘了這天應該保持靜默。
好，在下個空檔做。

每天度過的許多空檔，不要忘記
有些是應該做為靜默之用。

糟了！這下忘了今天應該斷食。
好，在下個空檔做。

斷食就不要餓肚子。

請下個定義，誰「不是」家人，
並說明為什麼不是。

請給個解釋，為什麼一顆馬鈴薯值一文錢，
而一粒鑽石值一百萬？

來，我們不要走動；就靜靜坐著，
度過下個空檔。

上一個空檔時你坐過的石頭
是平滑的，還是粗糙的？

集中。
抓住要「點」了嗎？

感官是滑溜溜的斜坡。
禁欲是在爬坡。

徒弟來到，看見有人在羞辱他的師父。
師父只是微笑坐著。
「師父，您為什麼要忍受如此的屈辱？」徒弟問。
「噓⋯⋯不要打擾我；你沒見到我正忙著
責罵這憤怒的人不該發脾氣嗎？」師父回答。

上一頁留白處有一苗燭火，
你見到了嗎？

你有停下來，對它沉思嗎？

在上一個留白處，我沒有寫東西，
因為那裡已經畫滿了許多山、許多河流、許多深谷、
許多森林、許多太陽、許多月亮、許多百合花。
你也有停下來，對著它們沉思嗎？
試一下，凝視那空白，沉思；
你就會看到那稀世的畫作。

什麼？好像聽到有人說
看不到自己要走的路？
即使他們有三隻眼睛可用？

有天我見到了一件最妙的事。
天上有個風箏，垂下一條線來栓住地球，
然後它拖著地球在太空中飛行，繞著太陽轉。
可是卻沒有人注意到！

在靜默中才言語。

在斷食中方進食。

你見到上個留白處的燭火嗎？
你有停下來對它沉思嗎？

今天，是否有一叢樹將它的花瓣撒在你行走的路面上？
你有報以微笑回應嗎？

有「欲望」就表示你覺得自己有所不足。
正因為外界的事物無法讓你變得圓滿無缺，
所以欲望才來個不停。

你內在的神是圓滿的。
從你內在的自我得到圓滿。

已經上去的人，才有下來的自由。
自己還不是精於上去之道的大師，
就不要下來。

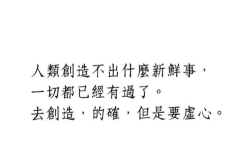

人類創造不出什麼新鮮事，
一切都已經有過了。
去創造，的確，但是要虛心。

不要用兵器去戳傷自己的靈魂！
所謂的兵器就是：憤怒、嫉妒、報復、暴力的念頭。

不要為問題而掙扎。
要學會如何不生問題的生活藝術。

如果你所追尋的自在，是一種要「遠離」什麼的自在，
或者是一種要「有」什麼的自在，
那你所謂的自在，還是有所依賴的。
自在。不用「遠離」什麼，也不用「有」什麼。
就是自在。

當下就是。不要老是在求「成為」怎樣。
能如此，你就得自在，得圓滿。

「是」就是不排斥任何作為。
當下就是。就去做。
不要「成為」。

整個世界都要依靠得自在者。
真得自在者就有如是能耐。

如果你還到不了那個境界，就擴大自己的心量；
把自己放大。

上一個留白處，你有沒有見到在那片草海中
的一朵花？你有沒有停下來，對它沉思？

把批評你的人，熱情地留在身邊。

能悔過，能補過，能坦然認錯，
還能欣然陪罪的人，才是強者；
他們會成為大人物。

如果你覺得整個世界是美麗的，
你就會成為美麗的人。
如果你是個美麗的人，
你就會覺得整個世界是美麗的。

靈性之檢測，在於情緒的淨化。

淨化情緒之檢驗，在於成功幸福的人際關係。
如果你能成功與他人相處，就證明你的靈性有進步。

愛神所造的眾生，神就會愛你。
神說，愛我嗎？去愛我的狗、貓、牛、蟻、象、人。

今天就能得到一個天啟。

心想事成絕對是可能的——
只需要用平滑柔順、不使勁的方式去做即可。

不用去尋找大師或是求他加持。
只管把自己磨練好，你自己要值，才能得。

什麼是所謂的培養人格力，
就是讓那些以前恨你的人現在愛你。

所謂的人格力就是：
憤怒的人來到你面前，會帶著微笑離去。

把別人對你的侮辱，當成是在促狹你。
就與他們開懷盡歡吧。

睡眠可不是靜默。靜默是有警覺的。
靜默是會說話的。靜默是能創造的。
靜默能讓旁人靜下來。

在你的面前，
如果別人的心不能自然靜下來，
那你就還沒有練過靜默。

所謂「心能轉物」是不成立的，
因為，心還是一種物質能量。
沉思什麼才是能夠轉心的那個靈我之力。

在上一頁留白之處，
你有沒有沉思我在上面寫了什麼？

不要靠希望。靠願力！

每個漩渦的中心都有個絕對靜止的點。
就安住在那裡。

你是每個漩渦中心那個絕對靜止的點。
就安住在自我之中。

肉體是軟弱的。
它抵不住心靈。
它一定會順從心靈的願力。發願吧！

活生生地過日子！
讓別人因為接觸到你，也能變得活生生的。

我在這一頁上寫的是無物。
沉思它空無一物的本質。

太好了！太棒了！我輸了。
太精彩了。

每當心觀察心，
心就消失了。

讓心寂滅，我才能「在」。

不要為使勁而使勁，
不要為不使勁而使勁，
柔順地滑進非使勁境地。

7

不妨頑皮。

拿張白紙當作一封信寄給弟子。

每日一頑皮，日日不厭疲。

不妨頑皮。把靜默
從窗口灑到過路人身上。

不妨頑皮。偷偷把一朵花
留在陌生人的門口。

不妨頑皮。在靜默之日，
寄一張白紙給你的朋友。

不妨頑皮。讓犯錯的員工罰錢，
再祕密地把罰款雙倍的錢存到他在銀行的私人帳戶中。

不妨頑皮。為敬愛的客人準備一餐精緻的美食，
當你受到稱讚的時候，
說你不懂烹調，功勞屬於一位你叫來幫忙的鄰居。

不妨頑皮。一文錢都不肯給那個無家可歸的人。
等在暗處，直到他睡著了，
才在他的被單下留一份慷慨的金額。

不妨頑皮。把啟發人心的引言和句子
寫在一些小紙條上，
把它們任意夾在圖書館的書中。

不妨頑皮。祕密地替人把欠債還清。

不妨頑皮。在與陌生人聚會時，
對你所精通的事假裝一無所知。
聆聽別人對此事的意見
以來自娛即可。

不妨頑皮。若你是一名官員，
以化名投書，去抨擊你自己的某些政策。
當被人引用來反對你時，竊笑以對。

不妨頑皮。寄一封匿名的仰慕信給不喜歡你的人，
列出對方有哪些優點。

不妨頑皮。送一束花
給昨天怒罵你的那個人。

不妨頑皮。假裝自己曾經使詐，讓利給對方。

不妨頑皮。假裝你已經不與某人往來，
然而不時在暗中幫助那個人。

不妨頑皮。趁人家不在時，
晚上潛入他們的後院，種下一株花。

不妨頑皮。在聖誕樹下
留下匿名的禮物。

不妨頑皮。若你真有醫病的神通，
就暗中為人醫病，然後否認是你出手。

不妨頑皮。若有人散播不利於你的傳言，
就開始散播對他有利的傳言。

不妨頑皮。在市場中為了五顆番薯的價格，
喋喋不休地大聲還價，
最後把這一小堆東西退回去──
在底下暗藏一顆鑽石。

不妨頑皮。與俊男美女為伍，
外表看似放蕩，
可是卻能守身如玉。

不妨頑皮。為人奉上牛奶——
但是端上來的是水。
想不到！人家喝了一口，
水居然變成了牛奶。
你假扮無辜，說原本端出來的就是牛奶。
絕不承認你把水變成了牛奶。

不妨頑皮。有人批評你，
就寫一首詩讚美他。

不妨頑皮。你想修復破裂的關係嗎？
每天匿名為他（她）送上一瓣花。
發願當對方以愛回應時，絕不告訴對方。

不妨頑皮。預言某人有美好的將來。
當它實現了，你就說不過是偶爾猜中而已。

不妨頑皮。把白紙當作信寄給弟子。

你能明白我昨天給你的信嗎？
你有練習守靜嗎？

不妨頑皮。當個醉人。被神的名字所醉。
將你喝下去的福音散播出去。

不妨頑皮。用有天女的說法，
引誘某人捨棄世俗。
然後在適當的時機引誘他捨棄有天女的想法，
讓他迷上神的美。

不妨頑皮。把你的狗叫作「象」。
向別人化緣，說你的象要吃很多的甘蔗
和其他食物才不會挨餓。
把你得來的分給窮人。

不妨頑皮。走近正在為某事而爭執的兩人身旁。
開始在地上找東西。
當他們問你在找什麼，
就說你有一枚銅板只有一面，另一面不見了，
請他們幫你找找看！

不妨頑皮。潛到河底去禪定。
如果有人問你為什麼在那下面待那麼久，
你就說：我精神失調，
一定要去數魚。

不妨頑皮。假裝憤怒，
繼續從事善行。

不妨頑皮。抓著雷電好像要劈下來，
卻只是為人照明。

不妨頑皮。讓自己因為偷心而被捕，
然後要求法院罰你待在冷酷無心的人群中。

不妨頑皮。當你處在冷酷無心的人群中而無心可偷，
就趁他們熟睡之際，把心植入他們。

不妨頑皮。在別人夢中的沙漠裡
種植美麗的果園。

不妨頑皮。如果你想在旅途中從事靜默，
卻與一群喧鬧的人同行，就掛個牌子在自己的脖子上，
寫著：暫時失去言語功能。
每個人都會同情你。

不妨頑皮。當有人問你是從哪裡來的，就拉著他爬上山。
讓腳下的都市反映在鏡中。
告訴問你的人，那就是你的國度的倒影，
所有你認識的人也都是從那裡來的。

不妨頑皮。宣布要演出最出色的交響樂。
走上指揮臺但不帶指揮棒，
然後指揮一曲靜默交響樂。

不妨頑皮。開個最大的玩笑。死去。
三天後起身，對著每個人大笑，
說：「哈哈，你們被我騙了！」

不妨頑皮。宣布要朗讀
取自世界各種經典的最佳集錦。
上台時不帶一本書,默默坐著一個小時,
最後才說:謝謝各位,
我衷心希望你們喜歡我剛才所選擇朗讀的部分。

不妨頑皮。學學這個例子。
我少年時期跟隨一位導師。
如果他發現自己所坐的火車到站時，
會有景仰他的人士和信徒
正帶著花環、拉著布條在守候，要向他致敬，
他就會提前一站下車，
然後改乘別種交通工具前往目的地。

不妨頑皮。宣布你要展出獨特的藝術品。
掛上許多鏡子，鏡框上寫著：
「你是獨一無二的藝術品，照照鏡子就知道了。」

不妨頑皮。用簡單的方式解釋複雜的事，
以至於人人都誤以為你是個沒文化、頭腦簡單的人。
出醜的是他們。

不妨頑皮。跟在不斷打結之人身後。
不停地在他背後幫他把結解開。

願你頑皮的念頭和行為，
讓你竊笑不已。

8

噓⋯⋯聽！
你有聽到上一頁留白處的音樂嗎？

以上留白處的文字，
是用夜間墨水寫的。
只有閉起眼睛才讀得到。
學學閉眼的讀術吧。

有兩種事該忘掉：
你幫助別人的事，
別人對不起你的事。

有兩種事要永遠記住：
你對不起別人的事，
別人幫助你的事。

世界再大，容不下兩位大帝共享。
一床被子雖小，卻夠兩名苦行僧人舒服地蓋著共眠。

鎖是語言結構學上一個術語，
它把所有詞「我的」固定於某個地方。
除此之外，它一無用處。

能懼神者，就無懼於其他。

不必在乎阻力。
繞道而行即可。

危機會過去。常態則永恆盛行。

有僕人之人，就會依賴僕人。
有百萬將士的帝王，依賴他人的程度是百萬倍。
宣布你能自主吧！

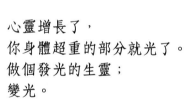

心靈增長了，
你身體超重的部分就光了。
做個發光的生靈；
變光。

輕佻的河流和沉穩的山巒，
哪有什麼相配之處。
可是，一個能滋養，另一個能撫抱，
所以這一對就只有對上了。

常常，仁慈為懷的神在施予；
桀驁不馴的人類卻排拒。

把別人對你的意見給解決了；
你對別人的意見也就解決了。

上面留白之處的天空，沒有任何墨水之雲。
你的心頭是否也同樣的清明？

東西就是東西。
不要讓東西成為念頭。

不要讓生理的狀況成為心理的狀況。

假裝依依不捨，讓人家覺得受到鍾愛。
私底下卻了無牽掛。

只要能自律，人生就輕鬆。
自律是真正的輕鬆。

神從不會說：我聽到你的祈禱了。
要在寂靜中去聆聽祂的回應。

神和上師的來到，是不會先預約的。

如果你還記著那份苦澀和憤慨，
舊的那段逆緣就還沒有斷。

愛的記帳方式是，
付出的記成正數，
留下來的記成負數。

不是所有的內在經驗都是永恆的經驗，
它們也不一定和心靈有關。
他們也許是在表皮之內的經驗，
但不是在心靈之內。

只要你還有苦澀和憤慨的記憶
你就仍然陷在那段情緣中。

夢境是扭曲的境象。
不要用扭曲的境象來預言未來。

閉起來！你才能打開。
打開，你反而會被關閉。

任何你想得到更多的東西，就把它給出去。

要追求的是，沒有感受的靜坐。
有感受，就是分心。

對自己任何的靈性體驗，要保持靜默，
能遵守這個規距，則體驗會更強。

人生帶來的包裝裡有苦有樂。
不論你怎麼換包裝，裡面一定仍然有苦有樂。

懂了你要問的是「什麼」，
就已經回答了半個問題。

對不起，我忙著打掃天空，
沒留意到會讓那麼多廢物掉到地上來。
那些打著心靈旗號，卻污染、弄擰、破壞了
現實世界人際關係的人，也一樣。

不能服侍、孝順自己上一代的人，
就不要冀望下一代
能服侍、孝順、聽從、尊重自己。

不能尊重自己師長的人，
就不要冀望自己能得到學生的尊重。

忠誠不是靠命令而來。它是掙來的。

如果敬是因懼而有，
寧可不要這種敬。

前生激怒過多少人，這一生就去撫慰多少人，
不要再激怒人；
你的業債才能還清。

烏龜和蟒蛇因為呼吸緩慢而長壽，
你當然能比它們更好吧。

即使在陰暗的早晨，雀鳥照舊歡唱；
你也行。

心中的蜘蛛網
要用靜坐的掃把來清除。

不為自己祈禱。
別人就會為你祈禱。

你第一次歡笑在哪裡學的,
就重遊那個學校吧。

你的笑容是預防、治療,還是事後補救?
如果是其中任何一種,就不算是笑容。

你能教我笑的正確技巧,
那我就能教你禪定。

你是否埋怨
神沒有回應你的祈禱？
你的祈禱相互矛盾，
拿定主意要祂聽哪一個，
祂會應你的。

有個安靜又免收租金的地方，
你應該經常去避居一段時間，
這地方就是你內心。

9

鑽石的靈是它的光芒。

靈魂的靈是愛。

有種酒名叫「我的」，是最會讓人喝醉的。
把你的酒杯反扣過來，說「您的」。

受到世間權貴者表揚，
對於心靈的修行者而言是一種侮辱。

你所懷的抱負，若不先到絕望的地步，
是不會完全實現的。

要成為完整的「你」
必須先經過苦行的歷練。

比起能登上高樓的人，
彎下腰來親吻人腳者，
才是更高的人。

胚石要經過切割，才能成為珍貴的鑽石。
金塊要經過火融，才能成為帝王的皇冠。

你所能做到世上最不自私的事，
就是讓自己的內在平和寧靜，
因為，只有你擁有的，
你才能給出去。

如果水龍頭滴水，
就留心聽那滴水之間的寧靜，
同時感謝神賜你一個滴水的龍頭，
幫助你禪定。

不要老是和問題戰鬥。
要依照生活的藝術來過活，
所以不再有問題。

痛苦是絕對消不了的，
只能被別的痛苦所取代。

大多數的歡樂，在取得的過程中，
不是要承受痛苦，就是要施以痛苦。

你能少尋歡，
就能從整體上為世界減少痛苦。

做個別人無從挑戰的人。
對你所有的想法都保持緘默。

瞧，有人能挑戰你的上一個想法嗎？

生命是一門講究精準的學問。
但是練達的人生是一門講究精巧的藝術。
做藝術家吧。

不求活得似帝王。
但學聖人過日子。

有很多門，只有小者能進，大者進不去。
做個小者，進得去的門就多了。

與批評你的人常相左右，
他們能保你不誤入陷阱。

人類是在哪次原始人的世界會議
簽下協約一致同意
花是美麗的？
可是這個共識又的確存在。

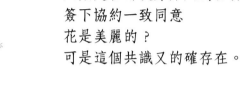

暴風眼不受沙塵刺激。
靜坐之人的內心
也不被外界的吵雜所干擾。

「教育」是一種
讓兒童喪失純真和智慧的
藝術和科學。

知識讓人得知；智慧讓人能行。

你有畫好構建自己人生偉業的藍圖嗎？

不說出來的約定，是最深刻的。

如果你說別人打擾你靜坐，
那代表你根本沒有在靜坐。

如果你想要，你可以得無限。
為何要追逐微不足道之物？
就怕你野心不大！

當你能做到
獅子把頭枕在你右腿上，小鹿枕在你的左腿上，
你撫摸著牠們的頭，
唯有這樣，你才算是一個完人。

人類只有聖人才是成人，
因為他們最像孩子。

黃金盛世來臨的象徵是，
生命學校裡教書的是孩子，
成人入學當學生。

如果你的靈感跑不出來，
你不要跑，
坐著不要動。

每個聖人都能成詩，
卻沒有幾個詩人能成聖。

不要盡談玄說理，
要做個哲人。

聖人默默無言，
極少數有福者才能聽清楚。

別吵……聽！
你聽見上一頁留白處的音樂嗎？

神的諭令
是刻一塊岩石上，
它藏我們面額後方的
一個洞穴中。
登上去之路很陡峭。

締造宇宙時，首先用到的材料是靜默。
你在上一個留白之處已經領略了。

沒點亮的蠟燭不能照路。
沒開悟的不能讓人開悟。

把神當成你的祕密情人。不要告訴任何人。

聖人總是會找罪人結伴，因為慈悲。

真能戒慾的人會與妓女結伴，
否則，若他的純潔不能感染，
他戒慾有何用？

醉心於解脫是一種癮，
成癮則終得解脫。

與聖潔之人為伍，是最佳療法。

心靈追尋，遠比心理設定來得強大。
前者永遠可以克服後者。

宇宙最終會分解，溶入靜默中。

你昨天有助人嗎？
如果你記得，而且回答「有」，
那你就沒有助人，
只是助長了你的傲慢。

通往寧靜和解脫的入口處何在？
就在字與字之間。
仔細找，進去。

比斷食更好的是，
有規律、有節制的進食。

比靜默不語更好的是，
發願只說有益、有度、愉悅、輕聲的言語。

百科全書，被無知者和知者所寫滿。
智者在寫第一個字之前，就停筆了。

唯有不為一己，
才能充實一己。

你有些生而有之的本能被壓抑著，
順著它，例如：
無私。

疾病是在消業債，
不要為病而憂愁。

受波濤顛頗之際，就往下潛。
深處沒有風浪。

若你沒有張開眼睛去看，寶石也會是廢物。
張眼看看散布在自己四周的美，
你就永遠不憂愁了。

人與人有爭吵是因為
看不見對方美好之處。

我在上個留白處
寫下的是
無上的真理。

寫下文字，只是為了
和寂靜的留白對比。
仔細看著留白處，
從那裡入門。

同時，向著你自己內在的美麗世界，
張開你的眼睛。
你閉上它們，就是睜開它們。

剎那與剎那波間的低谷，
就是潛入永恆之處。
潛下去。

寫在紙上的字與字之間，
就是呼吸之間的停頓。

孩子們，原諒大人吧。
因為，他們也不比你們懂事。

你究竟是在助人，
還是藉機炫耀自己是富人？

11

宇宙的第一個建築
是寂靜。

在上個留白處，
你已經見證它了。

你在上個留白處禪思時，
沒有分心？靜默壓過一切？
恭喜你了。

沒人愛你？
做個可愛之人。

你沒有磁力？
磁化自己。

無論你怎麼重複大聲疾呼，
都沒人理會你？
學著去輕聲地說、斯文地說、溫柔地說、親切地說。
像神。

沒人稱讚你？
恭維別人。

有成就而傲慢的人，需要百萬衛士來保護他的成就。
因謙遜而有成就的人，自有百萬守護者來照顧他。

開始像神一樣地自謙。

神創造了整個宇宙，卻謙遜地隱藏自己，
以致連世人都懷疑祂可能根本不存在。

往昔先知所秉受的天啟，
也可以由你傳達。

即便你寫出詩篇的文句，
足以覆蓋整個大地，
比起神的宇宙詩篇，
又算得了什麼？
對自己的任何創作，都要心懷謙遜。

終其一生只活在感官世界之人，
猶如一名王子，由出生至死亡
只坐在窗前往外望，
從不知他宮室內在的華麗。

珍珠中沒有智慧，
聖人之智慧中卻有珍珠。

別人迴避你？
美化你的心靈。

唯有神才能造化，我們都是所造之物。
而我們所造的更僅是槽粕。

戴著神色眼鏡之人
看一切物件、眾生，都只見到神。

當你覺得他人的干擾分貝上升，
就進入深沉的靜默。

蠟燭會被微風吹熄，因為它是外物所點燃。
暴風不能吹熄螢火蟲，因為它的光芒是內在的。

太陽不會因為你吹它而落。
真正偉大的人，不會因為被人詆毀而黯淡。

太陽不會因為你吹起地球上所有的火而升。
偉人要時間到了才會現身。

力量生自心甘情願的磨練。
放縱則是在消耗。

詩人用文字來奏樂。
音樂家在琴弦上展舞藝。
畫家唱的是色彩的歌。
雕塑家是形狀的音樂家。
建築師在空間的舞台上弄舞。
作家雕鑿的是文字的圖像，
構建的是思想的巨廈。

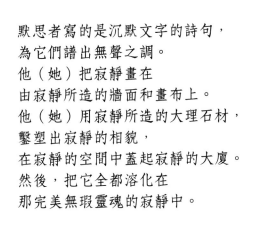

默思者寫的是沉默文字的詩句，
為它們譜出無聲之調。
他（她）把寂靜畫在
由寂靜所造的牆面和畫布上。
他（她）用寂靜所造的大理石材，
鑿塑出寂靜的相貌，
在寂靜的空間中蓋起寂靜的大廈。
然後，把它全都溶化在
那完美無瑕靈魂的寂靜中。

你怎麼能靠施肥和澆灌，
來讓月亮盈實？
任何東西都有它自然成長的步驟。

你說某人工作時整天在心中咒罵你？
你多幸運，有人整天念著你哪。

身體有何美麗，每個開孔都會滲漏！
——若你僅僅是身體。

身體何其美麗，神都會住在其內
——若你是個靈性之人。

不蓋住，蒸汽就逃逸無踪。
蓋住了，它就推得動巨大的機械。
人的思想和言語，不蓋住的和蓋住的，豈不更是如此？

能推動機械的蒸汽，
若沒有水和火的力量結合，則生不出來。

錄音機不會比人類先開悟，
即使它能記得更多也是徒然，因為它
不理解、不靜思、不實踐。
若人不理解、不靜思、不實踐，也是一樣。

有韌力的，即使傾跌也是有萬鈞之力。
所以瀑布能驅動磨坊。

火向上燒，
想要觸及它的親人，太陽。
你也有此嚮往嗎？
讓心靈的火焰向上燒，觸及神？

婦女要得到聖母的加持，
就視自己為她之轉世，
然後去感受自己的心態。

若你要得到聖母的加持，
學會尊敬大地。

若你要得到聖母的加持，
學會尊敬水。

若你要得到聖母的加持，
尊敬賜予你母親之乳的牛隻。

不要只做個會招呼客人的主人。
要讓他們存著朝聖的心情前來。

把自己的宮殿燒毀，或是拆掉自己的茅屋，
還不能算是出家。

怎麼處理難以克制的欲望？
什麼也不做。
不自責，不縱容。不否定，不肯定。
無動於衷，跳躍的狗自然會靜下來。

靈能在攪動怎麼辦？
什麼也不做。隱藏，吸收。

該如何求取上師的關注？
不要去求。
去完善自己。

最困難的捨，是捨棄知識。
唯有能捨，智慧才會露曙光。

假裝有所依戀，
才不會傷到那些把依戀當成是愛的人。
然後慢慢把他們的依戀
轉化成愛。

因為心靈有意志，
肉體才是軟弱的；
它永遠不敵心靈的意志。

當時間變成了沒有分割之流，
你就成為不朽。

仇恨是一種最強力的執著。
越少執著就越少恨，
也就越多愛。

讓心靈從物質獨立出來。

你在上個留白處禪思時沒有分心？

靜默壓過一切？

恭喜你了。

你翻到上一頁的留白處時，
心是否澄淨如天空？

我問那蜿蜒的流泉：你為何在林中遊蕩？
它汩汩地回答：我四處找尋一位
他足下的沙粒，可以為我理性的清明
帶來靈性的清純。

靈感不流暢？
與河流為友吧。

覺得被困在地面？
讓你的心成為鳥翼，與天空為友吧。

脾氣火爆？與月亮為友吧。

我問雷電：你為什麼閃光？
她答：我閃光，是為了要顯示
心中的迷霧再厚，靈光也可以透出來。

自覺淺薄？靜思海洋吧。

願你在開悟前，能引領眾人朝向解脫。
願你在開悟後，能引領眾生朝向解脫。

自覺心冷？與火為友吧。

沒有成長？
每天為一棵神聖的植物澆水。

應該從什麼時候開始幼兒教育？
在受胎三年以前。
幼兒的教育應該什麼時候結束？
在成胎九個月之後。

若你小題大作以鼠丘為山，
請確定在它谷中造一條河
來灌溉世界。

逃避是一種最強力形式的執著，
它抓得最緊。避免逃避。

挖個山谷，你就造了山。
建一座山，山谷自然來到。

我們是自己的天使，我們是自己的魔鬼。
每當我們遇到別人，就是遇到自己。

若我們真的遇到了自己，
就再也沒有孤寂。

河流不需要斧頭來斬平在河道中的樹木。
如果你懂流水的道理，你也不需要斧頭。

要把不成調的雜音變成交響樂，
就把這些音符重新排列組合即可。

在烏鴉的聒噪聲中，
聽見杜鵑低鳴的樂聲。

海水，提煉了，就化為淡水。
罪人，淨化了，就成為聖人。

學會在毫無滋味中嚐到滋味。

集合歷史上所有的帝王，
也不能教給聖人一個字。
一位托缽僧人，
就足以教導所有過去
和未來的帝王。

音樂大師
可以用一個錫罐奏出最美的曲聲。
其他人以為是稀泥的，
在香精大師的手裡可以製成香水。

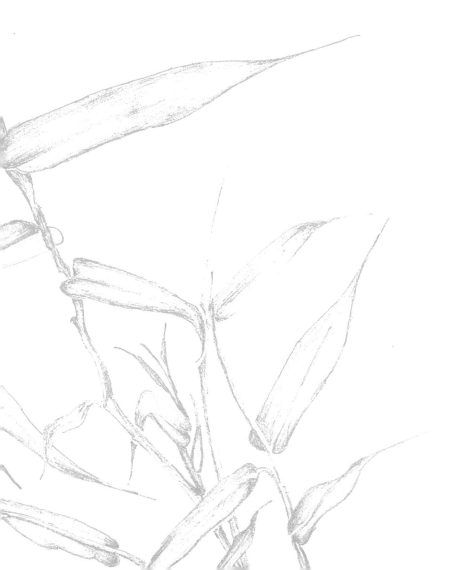

從惡臭中聞到芳香。

用光打造出來的劍，
不會輸給用鋼打造出來的劍。

善繪者即使用沙都可以作畫。
真能救人者，懂得用致命毒藥調出救命的藥劑。

能造聖者，
可以把人們所不齒的罪人，
感化成最聖潔的聖人。

真正求道之人，
住在烈火形成冰川中的洞穴內，
每天在火焰波浪的河流中洗浴。

你能和懷孕的母親懂得一樣多，
才能為人師。

你能和胎兒懂得一樣多，
才真能為人徒。

我們知道，北京一隻蝴蝶拍一下翅膀，
可以在華盛頓形成風暴。
一個人心中閃過一個憤怒或嫉妒的念頭，
會怎麼影響到整個人類的歷史？
恐懼會引來危機。

那些主張
世上的樹木、花草、乳鹿、河流
都是為了他們而存在之人，
應該問問女士們，
真是如此嗎？

是否有一個月亮能照亮夜晚，
又有另一個使夜晚變得黑暗？
是否有一個太陽造成白日，
又有另一個撒下夜晚的罩子？
為什麼你老是在找分歧和劃分之處？

若你非發怒不可，就對著你的憤怒發怒吧。

無懼的意義不是勇敢。它應該定義成：
慈愛、勿傷生。

跟樹學習。
遭人砍斫，仍然保持寧靜，
——《奧義書》

猴子伸手到裝滿杏仁的瓶中。
牠的拳頭裡握滿了果子，卡在瓶頸中抽不出來。
牠該如何脫身？
放手就可以脫身了，果子晚一點還是可以倒出來的。
放手，我這隻猴子。

世界要靠著植物呼出來的氣，才能活命。
眾生的心靈吸收了綻放的花朵而美麗。
你呼出來的是什麼？
你綻放了什麼出來？

我問杉樹：
你如何不停地為整個世界呼出新鮮的生命？
杉樹問我：請定義什麼是
「如何」。

我問茉莉花：
為什麼你不停地綻放出美來裝飾世人的心靈？
茉莉花問我：請定義什麼是
「為什麼」。

當噪音能被降服，
惡魔也不復存在。

收進來的，不是被用盡就是失去。
捨出去的，會結了成千上萬的果子回來。
哪個比較合算？

對現有世界感到厭倦？
下一個留白處所隱藏的世界，
是更聖潔、更寂靜的。
去「發」「現」它。

我問：「蓋婭」女神之牛：
你那永不竭盡、源源不絕的恆河牛奶，
是儲存在哪裡的？

她回答：在我母性的心念中。

乳牛、大地、神、母親、河流，
若說這些不是同義詞，
我們的心靈就是朦朧不清的暗夜。

謙遜才是真力量。
其他的力量都是軟弱的。

譯注：蓋婭（Gaia）是希臘神話中的大地母親。

斯瓦米韋達雋言原文

1

*Spaces between written
words are pauses between
breaths.
Learn to read the
inscriptions that are in
blank spaces.*

TIME is a person like yourself.
Negotiate with him.

To reach your goal quickly,
go in the opposite direction.

If you seek victory, surrender!

The HARD are weak and brittle;
the gentle are resilient, tensile, strong.

God makes day and night both;
why do you need to choose only one.

When faced with a conflict of choices between
two opposites, have both; you will become a
bi-polar magnet.

Knowing much is ignorance;
knowing only One is wisdom.

The lustful caress only limbs;
those who love caress minds. Be a lover.

The already feminine have nothing
more to learn; the flower need not seek
the status of a stone.

Page 14

If you are male, learn to
be feminine. If you are
female, remain feminine.

Page 15

Cataclysms are
readjustments for renewal.
Know this and you will
emerge as a fresh flower after
a stormy night.

Page 16

Radha played at being Krishna;
Krishna cannot play Radha fully.

Subtle pride is sinister;
one does not know where it lurks.
Seek it out and vanquish it.

Let your pleasure be in that you caused
pleasure in the Other. To seek pleasure
in return is to cancel what you gave.

Do not keep a count of your gifts,
Only keep account of what you owe.

Learn the dances of the subtle body.

Wish to overcome fear?
Cease to be a cause of visiting death upon any creature.
Discover your kinship even with an ant.

Exude fragrances of your mind wherever you walk.

Play your laughter, too, in the symphony of God's
guffaws of open spaces.

When someone is just at the verge of becoming
hostile, befriend him.

Do not compete with others.
Only do your very best.

In Rishikesh we know
how to dye your
clothing. But we dye
only saffron.

Do useless things
often, for example, smile,
or meditate.

Learn to read the inscriptions that
are in blank spaces.

Too much striving leads to failure.
Are you striving too much?

Be effortless in your actions. Glide. Flow.

Be the first to voice what might be

someone else's criticism of you.
Then s/he will have nothing left to say.

When you have an uncontrollable urge to speak,
that is the time you must go silent.

There are no irreconcilable conflicts.

Shall I take it, or shall I leave it?
YES.

Is it white or is it black?
YES.

Is it vice or is it virtue?
YES.

Did it happen this way or the other way?
YES.

When you are torn between
two mutually exclusive options,
you are missing a third one in
which the two can be
assimilated making 3=1.

Desires are memories of
past experiences. Would it
not be boring to go through
them again?

Is my religion right, or his? YES.

Do not suppress anger. Only, do not have it.

Again, learn to read the inscriptions that are on empty spaces.

Do not look for the company of a dwarf only so you can feel tall.

Indulgence is defeat.

Ascesis is triumph.

Do no work unless you make it a pleasure. Have fun!

Be happy, for no reason, from no cause, at all times.

Better than happiness is serenity.

Did you learn to read the inscriptions that are on the empty spaces?

2

Page 27

Ecstasy is nothing.
Seek serenity.
See it in the preceding
space.
Contemplate there.

Page 28

A single sip of orange juice can send you
into mystic ecstasy: just concentrate on it.

Between ingress and egress is the pause that is the
open door to infinity.

How do you spell 'world' ? Y-T-I-N-I-F-N-I.

How to transcend the world?
Reverse the spelling above.

Page 29

Not even the smallest flame has ever
feared thickest darkness in vastest hall.

Do not try to know it all.
Cease not till you know the All.

Cling to the feet of a Master who can
introduce you to yourself.

Whatever impression you get
at the last space that was left blank,
gaze at it and contemplate.

River stands still when the shores flow.

The rich eat much
but taste little. The
poor eat little but taste
much. The latter are
the richer.

Today I had a dreadful
near-death experience: I
forgot to weave my prayer
into my breaths for as long
as three respirations.
Then I re-incarnated.

To climb to mountain peak,
get down to the bottom of the valley and
you will have reached the summit.

Wisdom needs few words.

Did you practice the silence of the last empty space?

Breezes need no passports; breathing
humans need no nationalities.

When will the golden age return?
For you, whenever you want.

One may live in personal dark ages even in the
Golden Age. One may live in a personal golden age even
in the dark ages.

Do you wish to conceal yourself from God?
Do you wish to Waterproof a wave?

Do you wish to hide away from God?
Do you wish to fireproof a spark?

Do you wish to deny the being of God?
Do you wish to have light deny the sun?

Do not seek to be a flower-rending storm.
Seek to be a fragrance-fetching wave.

Page 34

Do you want a
child to listen to you?
Get down on your
knee, your eyes to
his face level. Then
speak clearly and
gently.

Page 35

Every weakness of a
person, group, nation, is a
weakening of some strength.
You cannot weaken a
weakness: Find the
strength that it is a
weakening of, then
strengthen the strength.

Page 36

The last empty space was the pause
between two breaths. You filled it with
your self-observation and awareness.

Did someone say,
"I do not believe in God?"
How wonderful.

It was by God's Grace that s/he
uttered the word, 'God'.
The rest of the sentence does not matter.

You have no business scolding a child when you are
angry. Scold, pretend to, when you are calm.

I saw someone trying to sweep darkness out
of a room with a broom. Not even the tiniest
candle got lit thereby.

Page 37

I saw someone getting angry at someone angry.
I said: Be angry with anger and demolish it.

Gulliver went to a city where it was against religion
to taste anything sweet. They said: We cannot taste
your sugar, but do describe what 'sweet' is like.

Gulliver went to an island where they
followed the Lord's words: LET THINE
EYE BE SINGLE. They blindfolded one eye
of a child immediately upon birth, and for
life. They asked Gulliver to describe what
the world looks like with two eyes.

What's the taste of the word 'God' in the mouth?
Sweetest ever.

Page 38

The Yogi went to a world
where everyone's third eye
was blindfolded. They asked

him to tell what the realities
looked like with three eyes,
but refused to remove their
blindfolds.

Page 39

When God created
the soul He looked for a
place to house it. So He
made mind.

Page 40

Do nothing unless you make it a vacation.
Enjoy!

What does the world look like with three eyes?
Without its three dimensions, without the fourcornered
squares.

Sorry I cannot write in the
next space; it is too full.
So enjoy its fullness and linger therein.

Hate said to Love: I hate you.
Love said to Hate: I love you.

Do find a way to frolic in the most serious matters.

Page 41

Mind is the purest, clearest,
most luminous, most peaceful place in the universe.
That is why God gave mind as dwelling
place to the soul.

Mind is like an ocean.
Stormy at the surface, calmest in the depths.

Dust shows up clearly on the crystal.
Our stains show on the mind.

Keep your crystal chandelier of mind lit.

Why suffer the insatiate
cravings?
Enjoy the ecstasies of
celibacy.

The painting on the last space is the
most beautiful I have ever seen. Enjoy!

Do not suffer loneliness; enjoy solitude.

Break out of your solitary prison cell by entering the
silence and solitude of a monastic cell.

There is a monastic cell in the mind. Enter.

Stop wearing yourself down with incessant travel.
Become a pilgrim.

The entire world is not enough for
two emperors to share. One blanket suffices
for two mendicants.
Seek sufficiency.

If my destiny is known to the stars,
to whom is the stars' destiny know?
I shall ask Him direct about my destiny.

When I ask God about my destiny,
He says: make thine own with thy acts.

You want the Lord to shepherd you?
Then first be as a lamb.

Page 48

A sip of celibacy
imparts greater satiety
than an ocean of
indulgence.

Page 49

Enter your name for
the sports of stillness.
Do not compete and
you will win.

Page 50

Why suffer pangs of hunger?
Enjoy the pleasures of fasting.

An oceanful of the proud does not equal
a thimbleful of the humble.

Blank out your learning and you will find wisdom.

Fools are often wiser than the learned.

Do not meditate in competition with others.
Be alone.

Page 51

Do not join the Metaphysical Gossips Club.
Be silent.

Appear dumb in the company of the ignorant.

Keep your love secret in the company
of non-believers.

Help others without revealing your identity as the
helper. Your power to help will grow.

Heal others without revealing yourself as a healer. Your capacity to heal will be enhanced.

Page 52

Sound of the letter S is soft and sweet even in the words "salt sea". Be soft and sweet even in the harshest and stormiest associations.

Page 53

If you see two persons quarreling, smile at both of them and say nothing. The mood will change.

Page 54

Smile at those who are scowling at you.

Sail on the river that flows up the mountain.

Dawn of wisdom occurs at midnight.

Letters of the alphabet are notes from the bugles of angels. Those who have ears let them hear.

Bees gather only honey even from the thornbush.

Some clouds rumble and some rain. Be a raining cloud.

If you perform a miracle, do so non-chalantly; then deny having performed one.

Advise, not seeming to advise,
and people will listen. Guide, not seeming
to guide, and they will be led.

The elephant that the ant carried grew wings.
The sky that the gnat swallowed became infinity.
Pray to become that elephant and that sky.

In cultures where wine is sacred,
the saints change water into wine. Where wine is not,
but the milk is sacred, they change water into milk.
What lesson do we learn from that?

Last night in your sleep, did you hear
the sound of a bud opening into a rose in
your garden, and the moon shouting
"bravo" and the stars laughing in
celebration thereof? Then you have
mastered meditation.

Kabir said an ant carried an
elephant and a gnat swallowed the
sky. When you see that happening,
keep quiet; and you will become as
that ant and that gnat.

Enlightenment has been postponed enough.
Now get on with it.

The person you are afraid of walking
towards you in the dark is also afraid of you.

Allay his fear and you will have conquered all
your own fears.

When you will have exhaled inwards and
inhaled outwards twelve breaths without
pause, you will have entered the Great
Reservoir.

Learn to enter by the gates whereof the
closing is the opening and the opening is
the closing.

God needing some entertainment
put up a magic show and staged a slapstick
comedy called the universe. And you take
it so very seriously.

Relaxed turtle will win the race,
the restless rabbit will lose it.

Silent sages are being heard even after a thousand
years. The voluble are quickly forgotten.

Seek to be forgotten, and you
will be ever remembered.

I have told you so many things.
If you find out God's secret name for Himself,
won't you please tell me.

4

Page 61

*Did you hear the silence
of your soul on the last
space?*

Page 62

For pearls of wisdom, dive deep.

Sometimes the wisest become foolish. Do not mistake their foolishness for some kind of wisdom.

Sometimes the foolish show great wisdom. Do not reject their wisdom as foolishness.

Sometimes what appears to be foolishness is wisdom. Be discerning.

A clown is an important part of a drama. So are we important in God's universe.

Page 63

What does God do? He writes poetry. What has He written? A single verse. The uni-verse.

Breathe slowly. What's your hurry?

Those who do not honour the womb, become catatonic.

Give way to your basic urges.
For example, give!

Give way to your basic urges.
For example, sacrifice!

Page 64

In the summer ENJOY, and
store the sun's energy.
In the winter, ENJOY, cool
down, slow down the
metabolism, to live longer.

Page 65

Give way to your
basic urges.
For example, go into
silence.

Page 66

Well done; you went into silence.

Be not hard like a rock. Be strong like water that
grinds down the hardest rock into grains of sand. Learn
the ways of water that is women.

If you must sunder a relationship, leave no pain
behind, carry no pain along.

If you must sunder a relationship,
let no karmic debts remain.

Do mines wear their own gems? Do raisins sweeten
themselves to taste themselves? The noble create only
gifts for others, the ignoble for themselves.

Page 67

If you have fallen in the mud you cannot put your hand
on the floor of the Taj Mahal to rise. You need to put
your hand in the mud to rise.

To be included among the devotees of God you must
appear an utter fool in the eyes of the world.

If the world thinks you intelligent,
you are not yet a devotee.

You need total initiative to practice inaction
—— says the Gita.

Be a gourmet Epicurean. Savour the flavour of God.

Page 68

If someone asks you
about God...
...pour His silence into
their ear.

Page 69

Perfect the art of laziness.
Sit. Stay seated without
moving a limb. Let not even
your mind wander. Be true
to a vow of laziness.

Page 70

Fools are smart. They get all God's attention.

The path to God is hard —— you say.
Is life in the world easy?

Seek a life of ease, the ease of God.

Did you ascend the flight of stairs on the last space?
How was your flight?

What you run towards will run away
with its back to you. What you turn
away from will follow you.

Go towards what you fear. The afeared and the fear
will become afraid of you.

Between the pleasure of pleasure-seeking and the
pleasure of pleasure-giving, the latter is by far the more
intensely pleasure-granting.

Even a grunt can be a prayer if addressed to God
alone. Grunt to God and see.

Whom God would save, him He slays.
Seek to be slain at God's hand.

God the Mother's milk is called white light of
wisdom.

Fear not loving.
Fear not-loving.

If there is light in thine eye
thy whole world is lit.

A day of silence a week grants you into infinity a
peek.

S/he cannot grant forgiveness who would not humbly
seek forgiveness.

Smooth the wrinkles of your mind to keep your skin
smooth in the old age.

If thou hearest the silence within thy soul,
thou can't hear no noises from abroad.

Did you hear the silence of your soul on the last space?

Love assimilated into equipoise is ambrosia.
Love without emotional equipoise is poison.
May there be no poison in your cup.

If you cannot think of God as a friend, be
His enemy and challenge Him to battle. He
will accept your challenge, and this way
you will get to see Him face to face.

5

Page 77

*When you pass the empty
spaces of your days, do not
forget those that are for
silence.*

Page 78

Did you shower in the upward flowing waterfall in the
last space? All silences are upward flowing waterfalls.
Bathe in them frequently.

A caged mind will turn the vast open spaces into
imagined prisons. The liberated saint, if imprisoned,
will free the prison wardens from their many prisons.
Be not among the imprisoned; be among the liberators.

Afraid of shadows?
Rest under the shades.

In the centre of every
whirling wheel there is an
absolutely still point.
Weary of the whirl?
Go to rest in the centre.

Page 79

The drunken brother of a disciple would refuse
to come to the master.
The master hung a board on his hermitage:
WINE SHOP.
The brother came, and was reformed.
When will you open your wine shop?

Wherever the mind goes, let it go, for God is there.

Let the mind rest in God right there
where it has journeyed to.

Be a traveler in the inner world. Do some
insightseeing.

Page 80

The noisy minds will go
into the silent forest, and
leave a disturbance behind.
The serene will still the
city centre.

Page 81

Pleasure is the
antidote to pain.
When in pain, create
a pleasure.

Page 82

Do not suffer what is there to suffer.
Enjoy what is there to enjoy.

When standing by a lake you miss the sea,
you are also missing the pleasure of the lake.

Sculptors never sculpt; they only unveil with a chisel
what they wish to reveal.
Chisel away, and unveil the kind of life you want and
the beauty you would like to live with.

Do not stand like a tall tree in a storm;
you will be uprooted.

Innocence is highest wisdom.

Before a flood, bend down like the reeds,
you will be preserved.

Defenselessness is the best defence.

Humility alone saves one's pride.

Are you caught in a storm?
Be still.
The storm is bound to pass.

A man even the size of a mountain
is a dwarf before God.

You first lived inside your
mother. Just imagine that if you
wish to gain wisdom with
regard to relationships.
You lived INSIDE your mother.

Only one who
knows the soul is
beyond the reach of
death's arm, beyond
the fear of death.

A scholar who can debate in ten thousand languages
is an illiterate before the Omniscient One.

Even if you were granted 36000 of gods' years to live,
you will still live in the dread of death.

The needles dance, the magnet sits still.
It is the "passive" magnet that activates.

The storm-churned sea is silent and still twenty feet below the surface. So also is the mind.

Dive into your mind.

In relationships surest way to lose is by winning.
Lose, and you will win.

The man in the mirror thinks you are his reflection.

If you make love speak from your eyes,
what other adornment do you need?

The ugliest can become magnetically attractive by thinking beautiful thoughts.

When the rosebush dropped fragrant petals on your path, did you bend down and thank it?

All work for money is
prostitution.
Work to provide a service.
Receive money for needs.
The two are not connected.

Mind does not matter;
soul does.
Body does not matter;
breath does.
Matter does not matter;
spirit does.

Clouds do not eat the grain they nurture;
trees do not eat the fruit; rivers do not carry sweet
water for their own benefit. For no reason whatsoever,
the great live only for others.
—Sanskrit verse—

OOPS, I forgot to keep my day of silence.
Okay, on the next space.

When you pass the empty spaces of your days, do
not forget those that are for silence.

OOPS, now I forgot my day of fasting.
Okay, on the next space.

When you fast do not go hungry.

Please define who is NOT a family member;
and why not?

Please explain why a potato is for a penny,
and a diamond is for a million?

Come, let's not walk; let us just sit quietly
through the next space.

Was the rock on which you sat in the last space
smooth? Or was it rough?

Concentrate. Got the point?

Senses are slippery slopes;
Celibacy is a climb.

The disciple came and saw someone abusing his Master. The Master sat smiling. "Master, why do you take such abuse?" asked the disciple.

"Shhh... Do not disturb me; don't you see I am busy scolding an angry man for his anger?" replied the master.

6

Page 95

*Did you see the candle
flame in the last space?*

*Did you pause to
contemplate it?*

Page 96

I did not write in the last space because of all the mountains, rivers, valleys, forests, suns, moons, lilies, blossoms painted on it.
Did you also pause and contemplate them?
Try, gaze at the space, contemplate;
you will see the master painting.

What? Did I hear someone say s/he is not seeing her/his way? With all three eyes at their disposal?

One day I saw something most interesting. A kite in the sky sent down a thread and tied it in the earth; then it flew the earth in space, heading it around the sun. But nobody took notice!

Speak only when you are in silence.

Page 97

Eat only when you are fasting.

Did you see the candle flame in the last space?
Did you pause to contemplate it?

Did a shrub drop and sprinkle flower petals on your path today? Did you smile back in acknowledgment?

"Desire" means feeling oneself incomplete. No
external object can complete you, hence desires are
recurrent.

God in you is complete.
Be complete within your self.

Page 98

Those who have
ascended have the
freedom to descend. Do
not descend till you are
a master of
the science of ascent.

Page 99

Nothing original can be
created by man; it has all been
done before. Create, indeed,
but be humble about it.

Page 100

Do not maim your soul with weapons, that is,
thoughts of anger, envy, vengefulness, violence.

Do not struggle with problems.
Learn the art of living a life in which no problems arise.

So long as you seek a freedom 'from'
and freedom 'to', your freedom is dependent.
Be free, not 'from' something, nor 'to'
something else...
Be free.

BE. Do not keep seeking 'to become'.
Then you are free, and complete.

From Being, no action can be excluded.
BE. ACT.
Do not become.

The whole world is dependent on the Free.
The Free have such capacity.

If you are not succeeding, increase your mental
capacity; enlarge yourself.

Did you see a flower growing in a sea of grass in the
last space? Did you pause to contemplate it?

Keep your critics close at hand affectionately.

Those who experience
contrition, undertake
expiation, openly confess, and
readily offer an apology,
are the strong; they will
become great.

If you perceive beauty in all
things you will become beautiful.
If your are beautiful you will
perceive beauty in all things.

The test of spirituality is in purity of emotions.

The test of the purity of emotions is in successful and
happy relationships. If you are succeeding in
relationships you are making spiritual progress.

God loves those who love His creatures. He says:
Love me? Love my dog, cow, ant, elephant, human.

A revelation can be had today.

One can accomplish absolutely anything one wants——
only if s/he goes about it gliding smoothly and
effortlessly.

Page 105

Do not seek a Master or his Grace. Only hone
yourself; make yourself deserving.

The meaning of cultivating personal power is:
those who hated you now love you.

The meaning of personal power is: those who came in
your presence angry went away smiling.

Take others' insults of you as practical jokes.
Have fun with them.

Sleep is not silence. Silence is alert. Silence speaks.
Silence creates. Silence silences.

Page 106

If in your presence
others do not go
naturally silent in the
mind, you have not yet
practiced silence.

Page 107

'Mind over matter' is
fake, for, mind is a material
energy. Contemplate the
power of spirit-self over
mind.

Did you contemplate on what
I wrote in the last space?

Do not wish. Will!

In the center of every whirl there is an
absolutely still point. Rest there.

You are the absolutely still point in the centre of
every whirl. Rest in self.

Flesh is weak.
It has no power to resist the spirit.
It shall do as the spirit wills. Will!

Live life live!
Let others too come live by touching you.

I have written nothing on this page.
Contemplate its no-thing-ness.

Hooray! Bravo! I lost.
How wonderful!

When mind observes mind,
mind vanishes.

Let mind be extinguished so that the self may Be.

Do not strive to strive,
Do not strive to not strive,
Smoothly slide into non-striving.

7

Page 111

Be naughty.

*Send a blank sheet as
letter to a disciple.*

Page 112

One naughty act a day keeps boredom at bay.

Be naughty today. Sprinkle some silence from your
window onto the passersby.

Be naughty. Leave a flower anonymously
at a stranger's doorstep.

Be naughty. On your days of silence
mail a blank page to your friends.

Be naughty. Fine an errant employee; secretly deposit
double the amount into his private bank account.

Page 113

Be naughty. Prepare an exquisite meal for a
beloved guest, and when you are complimented,
say that the credit goes to a neighbor you called over
as you do not know to cook.

Be naughty. Refuse to give a penny to a homeless
person. Wait in the shadows till he falls asleep,
then leave a generous sum under his sheets.

Be naughty. Type some inspiring quotations and
sentences on little slips of paper and leave them
randomly in library books.

Be naughty. Pay off some one's debt secretly.

Page 114

Be naughty. In a party play
ignorant in an area of knowledge
you are a specialist in. Others'
observations on the subject will
provide you much entertainment.
Enjoy yourself!

Page 115

Be naughty. If holding a public
office, write an article under a
pseudonym criticizing some of your
policies. Chuckle when it is quoted
against you.

Page 116

Be naughty. To someone who dislikes you send
anonymous letters of adoration listing his/her good
attributes.

Be naughty. Send a bouquet of flowers to someone
who abused you yesterday.

Be naughty. Profit someone,
and pretend to have cheated.

Be naughty. Pretend to have severed a relationship,
and keep benefiting the person secretly.

Be naughty. Sneak into some body's backyard at
night and plant a flower while they are away.

Page 117

Be naughty. Omit the giver's name on your gift to be
opened under the Christmas tree.

Be naughty. If you have healing power, heal someone
unacknowledged. Deny having done so.

Be naughty. Start spending good rumours about someone who is spreading bad ones about you.

Be naughty. Haggle and shout and be garrulous in the marketplace over the price of five potatoes, and finally return the little heap——
with a hidden diamond at the bottom.

Page 118

Be naughty. Surround yourself with beautiful men and women; appear licentious.
Remain celibate and untouched.

Page 119

Be naughty. Offer someone a glass of milk—— but give water! And lo! After the first sip the water turns into milk.
Play innocent, and say that you had given him milk.
Never admit you changed water into milk.

Page 120

Be naughty. Write a poem in the praise of someone who criticizes you.

Be naughty. Do you want to win back the amity of someone who is alienated? Send him/her an anonymous flower petal daily. Vow never to tell him when s/he returns with love to you.

Be naughty. Prophesy something beautiful about some one's future. When it comes true, say that it was just a guess that came true coincidentally.

Be naughty. Send a blank
sheet as letter to a disciple.

2
4
2
/
2
4
3

Page 121 Did you understand my letter of yesterday? Did you
practice silence?

Be naughty; Be drunk. Be drunk on the name of
God. Spread the gossip that you drink.

Be naughty. Lure someone away from the world with
a promise of heavenly nymphs.
In due time lure him away from the thought of heavenly
nymphs, with the beauty of God.

Be naughty. Name your dog 'elephant'. Go about
asking for sugarcane or whatever for, you have to feed
your elephant who will other-wise starve.
Distribute what you get to the poor.

Page 122 Be naughty. Go near two people who are
fighting over some issue. Start searching for
something on the ground. When they ask what
you are looking for, say that you have only one
side of a coin and have lost the other side, and
would they please help you look!

Page 123 Be naughty. Take a dive and
sit down in samadhi at the
river bottom. If someone asks
what were you doing down
there so long, say: I have a
compulsive disorder to count
the number of fish.

Be naughty. Pretend to be angry;
keep doing kind and benevolent deeds.

Be naughty. Grab lightning as if to strike.
Then only illuminate.

Be naughty. Get arrested for stealing hearts.
Ask the court to punish you by placing you among the
heartless.

Be naughty. When you are placed among the
heartless and there is nothing to steal, plant hearts into
them while they sleep.

Be naughty. Get into people's dreams of deserts and
plant there beautiful orchards.

Be naughty. If you wish to practice silence when
traveling among noisemakers, hang a sign around your
neck: temporarily speech impaired.
Everyone will be in sympathy with you.

Be naughty. Take someone along—— who asked where
you are from—— and climb a hill. Let the city below
reflect in a mirror. Tell the questioner that is the
refection you are a citizen of, and so is everybody else
whom you know.

Be naughty. Announce a performance of the best
symphony ever written. Climb up the podium sans a
baton, and lead a symphony of silence.

Be naughty. Play the ultimate joke. Die.
Get up three days later. Laugh at everybody
and say "ha ha! I fooled you!!

Page 126 Be naughty. Announce a Reading of the Best Selections from World Scriptures. Arrive at the stage sans a book and sit in silence for an hour. At the end, say: Thank you, and I do hope the selections read were to your liking.

Page 127 Be naughty. Follow this example. I had a mentor in my teenage years. If he found out that at the railway station of his destination he would be received by admirers and followers with special honours, garlands, and banners, he would get off at the preceding station, and take a different vehicle to where he would stay.

Page 128 Be naughty. Announce a unique art exhibit. Hang up mirrors, with inscription on the frame, "you are a unique work of art; see in the mirror".

Be naughty. Explain complex matters in such a simple way that everyone mistakes you for a unlettered simpleton. The joke is on them.

Be naughty. Walk behind someone who keeps making knots. Keep un-knotting behind his back.

Hope your naughty thoughts and acts have provided you with a lot of chuckle.

8

Page 129

Hushhhhh.... Listen!
Did you hear the music in
the last space?

Page 130

The writing in the above space
was inscribed in the ink of the night.
It can be read only with eyes closed.
Do learn the art of closing the eyes to read.

There are two things always to forget:
the good you have done for others,
the wrongs others have done to you.

There are two things always to remember:
wrongs you have done to others,
good that others have done to you.

The whole earth is insufficient for two emperors to
share. Two contented monks can share a blanket
and sleep comfortably.

Page 131

A lock is a term in syntax; it keeps the word 'my' in
place. Besides that it is a useless entity.

The God-fearing fear none else.

Be indifferent to resistances.
Bypass them.

Crises pass. Normalcy reigns perennial.

A person with a servant is dependent on him.
A king with an army of a million is a million times
dependent. Declare your independence.

Spiritual growth will
invariably reduce your
physical excess weight. Be
a being of light; be light.

What match can there be
between giggling river and
sombre mountain. Yet, one
nourishes; the other cuddles;
and the twain remain
entwined.

Oftentimes God in His benevolence proposes;
humans by their resistance dispose.

Solve the problems others have with you;
the problems you have with them will be solved.

The sky of the above space simply did not draw any
ink-cloud. Your mind, too, remained as clear?

Let things be things.
Let things not become thoughts.

Let not body-conditions become mind-conditions.

Pretend to be attached deeply, so others feel loved.
Be a secret renunciate.

Ascesis alone confers ease in life.
Ascesis is the true ease.

God never says: I have heard your prayer.
Look for silent signs.

God and Guru do not come by appointment.

A past bad relationship is not yet broken off if you
still remember its bitterness and anger.

In the book of love what
is given away is entered
as a plus; what is retained
is entered as minus.

Not all internal experiences
are experiences of eternity,
nor are they necessarily
spiritual. They may be
internal to the outer layer of
skin, not to the soul.

So long as you remember bitterness and anger you are
still in a relationship.

Dreams are distortions. Do not prophesy from
distortions.

Shut up! And you will open up. Open, and you will be
shut.

What you want to receive more of, give that.

Seek a meditation free of experiences; they are distractions.

Maintain the rule of silence about your spiritual experiences, and they will intensify.

Life comes in packages of pain and pleasure. You may exchange one package for another, but the pain and pleasure content will not change.

Know WHAT your question is; that is half the answer.

Sorry I was busy sweeping the sky;
did not notice all the debris falling to the earth thereby.
So do they who stain, strain, spoil worldly relationships
in the name of spirituality.

Those who have not
served, obeyed, listened to,
honoured their elders should
not expect to be served,
obeyed, listened to, honoured
by their offspring.

Those who have not
honoured their teachers
should not expect to be
honoured by their students.

Loyalty is not demanded; it is earned.

If to be respected means to be feared,
it is far better not to be respected.

Soothe as many in this life as you have ever irritated
in the past lives—— and irritate no more;
your karma will be paid off.

The turtle and the python breathe slowly, and live
long. Surely you can do better than them.

Birds can sing even on cloudy mornings;
so can you.

Cobwebs of the mind are cleared
with the meditation broom.

Pray not for yourself.
Then others will pray for you.

Re-visit the school where you had
learnt your first laughter.

Is your smile a prevention, a therapy, or aftercare? If
any of these, it is not a smile.

Teach me the correct technique for smiling,
and I will teach you meditation.

Do you complain that God
has not listened to your
prayers? Make sure which
ones of your contradictory
prayers you want Him to listen
to; then He will.

Retreat regularly at a
quiet place where you
have to pay no rent——
your heart.

9

Page 147

*A diamond's soul is its
brilliance.*

Soul's soul is love.

Page 148

The wine called 'mine' is the
most intoxicating—— Turn your wine
glass over with the word 'thine'.

To be honored by those of secular power is
an insult to a spiritual seeker.

Not till your aspiration reaches the level of
desperation will it be fully realised.

To become fully You,
you must go through ascesis.

Page 149

Between one who climbs a skyscraper
and one who bends down to kiss the feet,
the latter is the taller one.

A crude stone must be cut to become a
precious diamond. To crown a king the
gold nugget from the mine must go
through fire.

The most unselfish thing you can do in
the world is to attain peace and stillness
within yourself, for, only what you have
will you distribute.

Page 150

If your faucet drips, listen to
the silence between the drips,
and thank God for dripping
faucets that thus help your
meditation.

Page 151

Do not keep battling problems.
Lead a life according to the art of
living, whereby problems no
longer arise.

Page 152

No pain is ever alleviated without taking
some other pains.

Most pleasures cannot be had without taking or
causing pains.

Reduce your pleasure-seeking; that will reduce
totality of world's pains.

Become unchallengeable.
Let all your propositions be silent ones.

See? Did anyone challenge your last proposition?

Page 153

Life is a precise science.
Be a scient Life is a precise art. Be an artist.

Do not live life kingsize. Live life saint——— wise.

The small can enter through many doors in which the
large will get stuck. Be small and many doors will be
open to you.

Keep very close company with your critics;
They save you from many pitfalls.

Page 154

In which pre-neanderthal
conference of nations did
all peoples sign a treaty
agreeing that flowers are
beautiful? But an
agreement there is.

Page 155

The eye of the storm
is not irritated by dust
particles. A meditator's
mind is not disturbed
by the loudest
cacophony.

Page 156

"Education" is the art and science of making children
lose their purity and wisdom.

Knowledge informs; wisdom enacts.

Have you made a blueprint by which you
build your life's edifice?

The unspoken agreements are the deepest ones.

If others have disturbed your meditation, as you said,
then you were not meditating.

Page 157

Why do you seek little measures of
things when infinity can be had for the
asking? Be ambitious!

Only when you will caress a lion's head
on your right thigh and a fawn's on the
left, you will be considered a completed
human.

Saints are the only adults of humanity
because they are the most childlike.

A golden age will dawn when children will
teach in the school of life and adults will
enroll as students.

Page 158

If you run short of
inspiration, do not run;
sit still.

Page 159

Poetry comes to every
saint; sainthood comes to
a few poets.

Cease
philosophising and
BE a philosopher.

Page 160

Saints have said nothing;
few fortunate ones have heard it well.

Hushhhhh... Listen!
Did you hear the music in the last space?

10

Page 161

*God's commandments are
engraved on a rock in a
cave behind the forehead.
The climb thereto is steep.*

Page 162

The first building material of the universe was
silence. You witnessed it in the last space.

An unlit candle illumines no paths; the unenlightened
cannot enlighten others.

Let God be you secret love. Tell no one about it.

A saint will always seek out sinners' company, out of
compassion.

A true celibate will seek out the company of the
prostitutes; otherwise, what use is his celibacy if his
purity cannot be infectious?

Page 163

Addicts will be drawn to the free,
and will gain freedom.

Company of the Noble is the best therapy.

Spiritual seeking is more powerful than
psychological conditioning. The former will
always overpower the latter.

The universe finally dissolves into silence.

Did you see the picture of the dissolution of a
universe in the last space?

Did you help
someone yesterday? If
you remember, and say
YES, you have helped
no one except added to
your pride.

Where are the
gateways to peace and
enlightenment? In the
spaces between words.
Look closely and enter.

Better than fasting is regulated
and restrained eating.

Better than silence of speech is the vow of
beneficial, measured, pleasant, low-volume speech.

The ignorant and the informed
both fill encyclopaedias.
The wise stop at the very first word.

Selflessness is the only way of self-fulfillment.

Follow your natural urges that have been repressed;
for example, become selfless.

Illness pays off karma;
do not sorrow at your illness.

When being tossed on the waves, dive.
There are no waves in depths.

Gems are trash if you open not your eyes.
Open your eyes to the beauty strewn all around you,
and you will never sorrow.

People quarrel only when they cannot
see the beauty that is in others.

Page 168

I wrote the
ultimate truth in
the last space.

Page 169

Words are written only to
juxtapose silent spaces. Look at
the spaces closely and enter
through.

Page 170

Also open your eyes to the beautiful worlds that are
within you. You will open them by closing them.

Between the waves of moments are troughs
for diving through to infinity. Dive.

Spaces between written words are
pauses between breaths.

Children, forgive the adults;
for, they do not know any better.

Were you helping someone or were you
showing off that you are rich?

Page 171

*The first building of the
universe was silence.*

*You witnessed it in the
last space.*

Page 172

No distractions from meditation
occurred in the last space? Silence reigned supreme?
Congratulations.

No one loves you?
Become loveable.

No one is drawn to you?
Magnetise yourself.

No one listens to you no matter how
loudly and frequently you shout?
Learn to whisper, gently, softly, kindly.
Be God-like.

Page 173

No one praises you?
Compliment others.

The successful proud require a million guards to
protect their success. Those who succeed through
humility have a million guardians to watch over them.

Start being God-like in humility and self-effacement.

God created whole universes and hid Himself, in humility, so the world wonders whether He even exists.

The revelations that were granted to the prophets of yore can come through you also.

Page 174

Even if you created a poem
whose verses filled the surface of
an entire earth, how much is it
compared to God's universepoem?
Be humble about all your
creativity.

Page 175

Those who dwell only in their
senses all their life are like the
prince who sat in the window
looking out, from birth to death,
and never saw anything in the
interior of his ornate palace.

Page 176

There is no wisdom in pearls,
but there are pearls in saintly wisdom.

Others shun you? Beautify your mind.

God alone is creative; we are all creatures.
All that we create is merely creaturely.

Those who have worn God-coloured glasses see only
God in all things and creatures.

When you find others' disturbances rising in
decibels, go into deep silence.

Page 177

A candle is blown off by a soft breeze because it was lit by another. A firefly is not extinguished in a windstorn because its light is inherent.

You cannot make the sun set by blowing at it. The truly great are not dimmed by others' calumny directed at them.

You cannot make the sun rise by blowing on all the fires upon earth. The great will rise in their own time.

Power comes from voluntary suffering. Indulgence drains.

Page 178

Poet plays music on words.
Musician dances on strings.
Painter sings in colours.
Sculptor is a musician of
forms. Architect dances on
the stage of spaces. Writer
chisels images of words,
erects edifices of thoughts.

Page 179

A contemplative composes poems of
silence-words and sets them to silencetunes.
S/He paints silence on walls and
canvasses of silence. S/He chisels and
sculpts images of silence from marble slabs
of silence; erects lofty edifices of silence in
spaces of silence. Then dissolves it all into
the immaculate soul's silence.

You cannot make the moon wax full by
throwing fertiliser and sprinkling water at it.
Any growth takes its own natural course.

Did you say that while at work s/he curses you
the whole day in mind? How fortunate you are;
someone thinks of you the entire day.

What a beautiful body whereof every opening
oozes!—— If you are merely body.

What a beautiful body wherein God has come to
dwell—— if you are a Spirit Being.

Vapour unlidded escapes into oblivion; lidded it drives
mighty engines. How much more so about human
thoughts and words, unlidded and lidded?

No vapour, to drive engines, can be formed without
uniting the forces of water and fire.

Tape recorders will not be liberated before human
beings; even though they retain more, they neither
comprehend, nor contemplate, nor yet enact. So also
the human beings who do not comprehend,
contemplate, enact.

Even a fall of the resilient is a mightly driving force.
A waterfall drives flour mills.

The fire burns upwards
attempting to reach its
kin, the sun. Do you
aspire the same way,
your spiritual flame
burning upwards to
touch God?

Page 183

If you wish to receive the Great
Mother's Grace, and you are female,
know yourself to be Her Incarnation,
and feel your sentiments accordingly.

Page 184

If you wish to receive the Great Mother's Grace,
learn to revere earth.

If you wish to receive the Great Mother's Grace,
learn to honour Mother Waters.

If you wish to receive Great Mother's Grace, revere
the cow who grants you maternal milk.

Be not just a host to entertain guests.
Be their place of pilgrimage.

One does not renounce by burning one's palace or
dismantling his hut.

Page 185

What to do with overwhelming desire?
Nothing. Neither denounce yourself nor
indulge. Neither decry, nor affirm.
Indifference calms a jumping dog.

What to do with surges of spiritual power?
Nothing. Conceal and assimilate.

How to get the Guru's attention?
Do not try to get it.
Complete yourself.

Renouncing knowledge is the most difficult
renunciation. Only by that wisdom dawns.

Pretend attachments so that
those who know no love other
than attachment are not hurt.
Then slowly convert their
attachments into love.

Because spirit has
will, flesh is weak; it
can never overpower
the spiritual will.

When time becomes an unsegmented flow,
you become immortal.

Hatred is the strongest attachment.
The less attachment the less hate,
the more love.

Declare independence of spirit from matter.

Page 189

*No distractions from
meditation occurred in
the last space?*

Silence reigned supreme?

Congratulations.

Page 190

Was the mind-sky clear in the last space
you passed through?

I asked a meandering spring: Why do you keep
wandering in the forest? It gurgled the reply: I wander
searching for one the dust of whose feet will add
spiritual purity to my rational clarity.

Inspiration not flowing?
Make friends with a river.

Feeling stuck in the ground? Let your mind become a
birdwing and befriend the sky.

Hot-tempered? Make friends with the moon.

Page 191

I asked Lighting: Why do you flash forth? She replied:
I flash to show that inspiration may burst through a
most clouded mind.

Feeling in the shallows? Contemplate the ocean.

May you guide numerous people towards Freedom

till you reach enlightenment. Thereafter, may you lead innumerable beings to the same.

Feel cold-hearted? Make friends with a fire.

Not growing?
Water a holy plant or a sacred tree daily.

Page 192

When does a child's education begin? Three years before conception. When is a child's education completed? At the end of the nine months of being a fetus.

Page 193

When you make a mountain out of a molehill, made sure that in its valley you also make a river flow to irrigate the world.

Page 194

Aversion is the strongest form of attraction and has the firmest grip. Avoid being averse.

Dig a valley and you create a mountain; build a mountain and a valley will come along.

To study the history of entire human culture all you need to do is to understand one single woman.

We are our angels, we are our devils.
We meet ourselves whenever we meet any others.

When we truly meet ourselves,
there is no more loneliness.

A river needs no axes to flatten the trees in its path.
Nor do you need any axes if you know to flow.

Make symphonies from cacophonies; all it takes is
rearranging the same notes.

Hear the undertones of a cuckoo's music
in a crow's cawing.

Seawater, distilled, is sweet.
A sinner, purified, is a saint.

Learn to find savor in the flavorless.

All the kings of history
have not a word to teach to a
saint. A single mendicant
will suffice to guide all the
past and future kings.

One who makes music will
made sweetest music from a
tin can. A perfumer makes
perfume even from the wet
earth others call mud.

Smell the fragrances in the malodorous.

A sword made of light cannot be
defeated by one made of steel.

One who paints will make a painting
even from sand. One who heals will mix a

life-saving potion form lethal poisons.

A saint-maker will make the holiest of
saints out of a condemned sinner.

Page 199 A true seeker lives in a cave inside of
glacier of fire and daily bathes in a river
that has flames for waves.

Know what a pregnant mother knows and you will
become a teacher of people.

Know what a fetus knows and you
will be a true disciple.

It is known that a single flutter of a butterfly wing in
Bejing may cause a thunderstorm over Washington.
What does a single flutter of anger or envy in an
individual mind do to the entire human history? Fear
causes dangers.

Page 200 Those who say that the
world and all its plants,
flowers, suckling fawns, and
rivers, were made for man,
should ask women if it is
really true.

Page 201 Is there one moon to
brighten the nights and
another one to darken
them? Is there one sun to
make the day and a different

one to cast the pall of the
night? Why do you keep
looking for divergences and
dichotomies?

If you must get angry, be angry at your anger.

Fearlessness does not mean bravery. It is to be
defined as lovingness and harmlessness.

Seek to be like a tree.
When being cut, remain silent,
—— says the Upanishad.

A monkey has put his hand into a jar full
of almonds. His fist filled with nuts is now
stuck in the jar's narrow neck. How
should he free himself? Release the nuts
that can be poured out later, and free
himself. Let go, monkey I.

The whole world lives by breathing
the exhalations of plants. All beings' minds are
beautified by assimilating the exudations of flowers.
What do YOU exhale? What do YOU exude?

I asked a Bunyan tree: How do you keep exhaling
fresh life for the whole world? The Bunyan asked me
the meaning of the word HOW.

I asked the jasmine: Why do you keep exuding beauty
to adorn the world's mind? The Jasmine asked me the
meaning of the word WHY.

When decibels will be vanquished, the devil shall
cease claiming existence.

What is gathered will surely
be spent or lost. What is
renounced will return bearing
millionfold fruit. Which is the
more profitable?

Tired of our present universe?
In the next empty space is
concealed a saintlier, more silent,
universe. Dis-cover it.

I asked the Gaia Cow:
Where do you keep stored you inexhaustible,
incessant-flowing Ganges of milk?

She replied: In my maternal mind.

Cow, earth, GOD, mother, river:
if these are not synonyms, our mind is a dark
befogged besmeared night.

Humility is power.
Any other power is weakness.

BH0046

瑜伽修行語錄：
雖然默默無言，卻又道盡一切
Sayings: saying nothing says it all

作　　者｜斯瓦米韋達‧帕若堤（Swami Veda Bharati）
譯　　者｜石　宏
責任編輯｜于芝峰
協力編輯｜洪禎璐
內頁設計｜劉好音
封面設計｜比比司設計工作室

發 行 人｜蘇拾平
總 編 輯｜于芝峰
副總編輯｜田哲榮
業務發行｜王綬晨、邱紹溢
行　　銷｜陳詩婷
出　　版｜橡實文化 ACORN Publishing
　　　　　臺北市 105 松山區復興北路 333 號 11 樓之 4
　　　　　電話：（02）2718-2001 傳真：（02）2719-1308
　　　　　網址：www.acornbooks.com.tw
　　　　　E-mail 信箱：acorn@andbooks.com.tw

發　　行｜大雁出版基地
　　　　　臺北市 105 松山區復興北路 333 號 11 樓之 4
　　　　　電話：（02）2718-2001 傳真：（02）2718-1258
　　　　　讀者服務信箱：andbooks@andbooks.com.tw
　　　　　劃撥帳號：19983379　戶名：大雁文化事業股份有限公司

印　　刷｜中原造像股份有限公司
初版一刷｜2019 年 7 月
初版二刷｜2022 年 7 月
定　　價｜420 元
Ｉ Ｓ Ｂ Ｎ｜978-957-9001-98-4

國家圖書館出版品預行編目（CIP）資料

瑜伽修行語錄：雖然默默無言，卻又道盡一切／
斯瓦米韋達‧帕若堤（Swami Veda Bharati）
作；石宏譯．－初版．－臺北市：橡實文化出版：
大雁出版基地發行，2019.07
272 面；21×14.8 公分．－（Bh；46）
譯自：Sayings: saying nothing says it all
ISBN 978-957-9001-98-4（平裝）

1. 瑜伽

137.84　　　　　　　　　　108009271

本書中文版權由作者委託台灣喜馬拉雅瑜珈靜心協會授權出版